Whether you prefer a snooty Siamese or a common alley cat, choosing any kitten should be done with a good deal of care. Accept a kitten only after it is properly weaned (about two-and-a-half to three months after it is born).

Its teeth and digestive tract are by then properly formed, and since you'll soon discover that the fastest way to a cat's heart is through its stomach, it will thank you for your patience in the years to come!

A KITTEN'S FIRST TWELVE WEEKS
(IN A NUTSHELL)

Although the rate of a kitten's development can vary somewhat depending on breed (Siamese and Burmese cats are quite a bit faster in every stage), most newborns follow the same growth pattern. By eighteen days, the kitten begins to teethe, its ears straighten, and it makes its first attempts to crawl. Soon thereafter, it will try to stand — however unsteadily — and weaning can begin. As soon as the kitten can stand steadily, it can be fed from a bowl. By twelve weeks, a kitten will begin to shed its "baby" teeth. Eye color will also begin to change by three months (all newborns are initially blue-eyed), and an adult coat pattern should be well-defined. Your kitten is now well on its way to becoming a cat.

Since a newborn kitten can't see for the first two weeks of its life, the nose serves as a natural "radar" that enables your pet to navigate its new world. At first competing for suckling space, kittens will eventually find the nipple that suits them best and leave the area with their own specific scent. Blind as a bat, even a one-week-old newborn will be able to find its way back to the nest if separated from its mother.

We remember being much amused with seeing a kitten manifestly making a series of experiments upon the patience of its mother. . . . The kitten ran at her every moment, gave her a knock or a bite of the tail; then ran back again, to recommence the assault. The mother sat looking at her, as if betwixt tolerance and admiration, to see how far the spirit of the family was inherited by her sprightly offspring. At length, however, the mother, lifting up her paw, and meeting her at the very nick of the moment, gave her one of the most unsophisticated boxes on the ear we ever beheld. It made her come to the most ludicrous pause, with the oddest little look of premature and wincing meditation.

Leigh Hunt

THE CAT BY THE FIRE

Three little kittens

They lost their mittens,

And they began to cry, *Oh, mother dear,*

What! Lost your mittens,

We sadly fear

Our mittens we have lost.

You naughty kittens!

Then you shall have no pie.

Mee-ow, mee-ow, mee-ow.

No, you shall have no pie.

TRADITIONAL RHYME

It's a very inconvenient habit of kittens

(Alice had once made the remark) that,

whatever you say to them, they always purr.

Lewis Carroll

THROUGH THE LOOKING GLASS

But you must not think we allowed our kittens to behave

badly. On the contrary, we tried all we could to teach

them good manners. But even so, they tore up an old pair

of Dora's shoes, they scratched the polished furniture, and

clawed the new leather for the delight of exercising their

pin-like nails. "Well, I told you kittens are mischievous,"

Nanny said. "And some are more mischievous than others."

Ernest Nister
THE THREE KITTENS

Quite early in life Sam, of course,

had learned to know his mealtime. . . .

He was particular almost to a foppish

degree in his habits, and he was no

thief. He had a mew on one note to

show when he wanted something to

eat; a mew a semitone or two higher

if he wanted a drink (that is, cold water,

for which he had a great taste); and yet

another mew — gentle and sustained —

when he wished, so to speak, to

converse with his mistress. . . .

Walter de la Mare

BROOMSTICKS

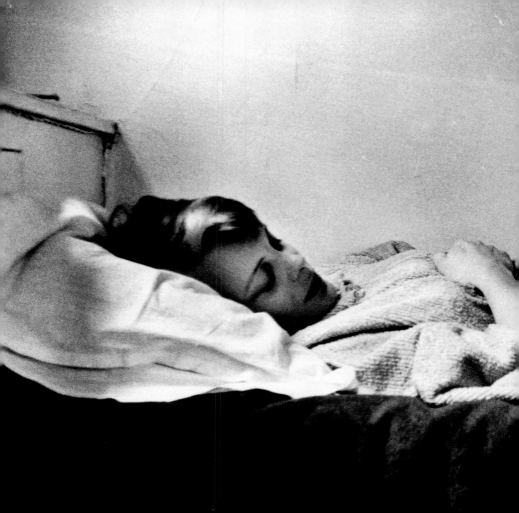

See the kitten on the wall

Sporting with the leaves that fall. . . .

But the kitten how she starts,

Crouches, stretches, paws and darts!

First at one and then its fellow. . . .

William Wordsworth
KITTEN AND THE FALLING LEAVES

His markings, month by month, became more beautiful, lines of autumn bracken colours with shapes which reminded me of currents on a quiet sea. True that at times his head, because of his youth, looked scraggy, even his body sometimes looked scraggy, but suddenly for some reason like the change of light, or of mood, he looked his potential. This kitten was going to be a champion cat. . . .

Derek Tangye
A CAT AFFAIR

Then I, the dangerous Kitten, prowl

And in the Shadows softly growl,

And roam about the farthest floor

Where Kitten never trod before.

And, crouching in the jungle damp,

I watch the Human Hunters' camp

Ready to spring with fearful roar

As soon as I shall hear them snore.

Anonymous

IN DARKEST AFRICA

CURIOSITY WON'T KILL THE KITTEN

Luckily for cat watchers, evolution has provided the feline species with a sense of curiosity that far outweighs its sense of fear. Although a new home is an adventure into the unknown — and therefore terrifying for any kitten — it won't take long before evolutionary instinct kicks in and he or she begins to explore . . .

and explore . . .

a n d   e x p l o r e !

CHAT À SA TOILETTE

If cleanliness is next to godliness, then cats must be among the most divine creatures on earth. Because of their spic-and-span second nature, kittens are toilet-trained in no time at all. As soon as a kitten can walk — at about four weeks old — the mother will teach him to use his litter box. If you are the surrogate mother, carry your pet to the box and make your tiny charge scratch with his two front paws in the sand. Your clever kitten should get the message in no time at all.

Like children, kittens can be smothered with too much affection.

If overhandled, newborn kittens — especially hand-raised orphans —

can become too dependent on human company in general or on one

person in particular. Accustom your cat to being left alone for

a few hours when it is still young (gradually, the amounts of time

can be extended). It's wise to feed your kitten before you go out

and to provide some playthings to stave off boredom (a catnip

mouse, for instance). Remember, a kitten is not a puppy.

I like little Pussy, her coat is so warm,

And if I don't hurt her she'll do me no harm;

So I'll not pull her tail, nor drive her away,

But Pussy and I very gently will play.

RHYMES FOR THE NURSERY (1839)

Gummitch was a superkitten, as he knew very well, with an I.Q. of about 160. Of course, he didn't talk. But everybody knows that I.Q. tests based on language ability are very one sided. . . . Gummitch alone knew the truth about himself and about other kittens and babies (that kittens turn into humans and babies into cats). . . . If you just rid your mind of preconceived notions, Gummitch told himself, it was all very logical. Babies were stupid, fumbling, vindictive creatures without reason or speech. What could be more natural than that they should grow up into mute sullen selfish beasts bent only on rapine and reproduction? While kittens were quick, sensitive, subtle, supremely alive. What other destiny were they possibly fitted for except to become the deft, word-speaking, book-writing, music-making, meat-getting-and-dispensing masters of the world?!

Fritz Leiber
SPACE-TIME FOR SPRINGERS

Pussy cat, pussy cat where have you been?

I've been to London to visit the Queen.

Pussy cat, pussy cat what did you there?

I frightened a little mouse under her chair.

 TRADITIONAL RHYME

Kittens have an ever-expanding program of play motifs that allows them to maintain their primitive hunting instincts even in the most domesticated environment. The trailing end of a piece of string will elicit classic stalking behavior followed by the "mouse pounce." The "bird swat" can be induced by the same dangling piece of string or any airborne insect such as a fly or butterfly. The "fish scoop" is also incorporated into many play motifs: just put some paper balls on the ground and watch your kitten pat and scoop up quite a game of soccer!

Our perfect companions never have fewer than four feet.

Colette

Always choose a kitten

that seems to interact with you.

Or at least make sure

it has a healthy relationship

with others in the litter.

Peter Neville, D.V.M.
Pet Behavior Therapist

I had rather be a kitten,

and cry mew

Than one of these same meter

ballad mongers. . . .

William Shakespeare

HOTSPUR IN *KING HENRY IV, PT. I*

As I was going to St. Ives, I met a man with
seven wives,
each wife had seven sacks, each sack had
seven cats,
each cat had seven kits: kits,

cats,

sacks

and wives,

how many

were there

going to

St. Ives?

Anonymous
AS I WAS GOING TO ST. IVES

To a
kitten,
every day
is a
holiday.

Janet Robinson

If work keeps you away from home,

you might consider acquiring

two kittens.

You will ease your conscience since they'll

be oblivious of their owner's departure.

Claire Bessant
CAT WORLD MAGAZINE

Although the mother usually provides a good deal of stimulation that helps her offspring develop normal "catlike" traits, human stimulation can be an effective supplement or even substitute (a must if your pet is an orphan). Although you don't want to overhandle your pets, handled kittens are less emotional and more playful than orphans or neglected kittens. Just as you wouldn't neglect a child during its first six years, a kitten's first few months are crucial in guaranteeing a happy cat — and a happy owner.

KITTENS VS. KIDS

Many feline-o-philes will argue that kittens

are far more practical than human babies:

1 A basket with a small cushion takes up less space than a crib.

2 Kittens don't need a lot of holding.

3 Kittens love to sleep.

4 Kittens don't cry as much in the middle of the night.

5 A kitten is toilet-trained in one or two lessons — and no diapers!

The trouble with a kitten is

t h a t

eventually it becomes a

c a t

Ogden Nash

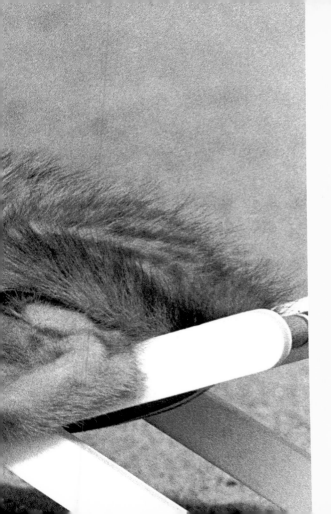

. . . Chessie was getting drowsier and drowsier. Very gently the train swung, rock-a-bye, rock-a-bye, and the wheels sang, softly, "clumpety-clump, now go to sleep. Clumpety-clump, now go to sleep." And so she did.

Ruth Carroll
CHESSIE